TABLE OF CONTENTS

Introduction...2
Absecon Lighthouse...5
Barnegat Lighthouse...7
Cape May Lighthouse...8
East Point Lighthouse...11
Fort Mott Lighthouse...13
Hereford Inlet Lighthouse...15
Sandy Hook Lighthouse...17
Sea Girt Lighthouse...19
Twin Lights of the Navesink...21

****
Remember,
   August is NATIONAL LIGHTHOUSE month.
****

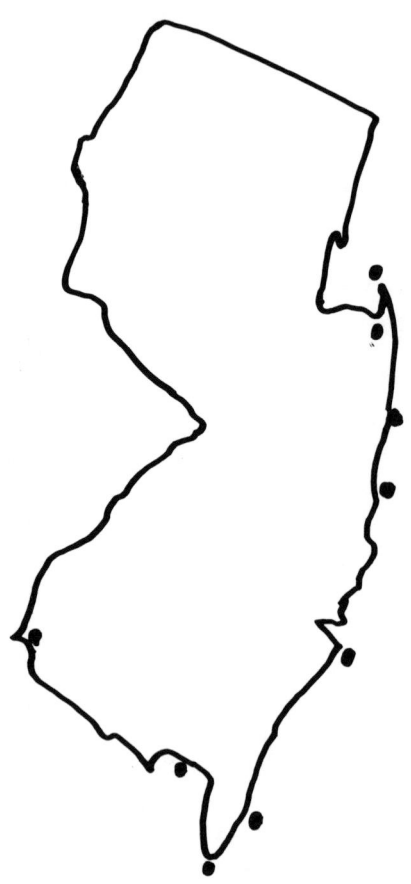

Copyright   1993   R. Marilyn Schmidt

All rights reserved. No part of this book may be reproduced or transmitted in any form or by any means, electronic or mechanical, including photocopying or recording, or any information storage and retrieval system, without permission in writing from the Publisher.

BARNEGAT LIGHT PRESS
PINE BARRENS PRESS
Box 305, Barnegat Light, NJ 08006

ISBN 0-037669-18-1

INTRODUCTION

A lighthouse brings to mind romance of the sea, sandy beaches, heroic acts, and ships at sea. The shoreline of the State of New Jersey, over the years, has had approximately 30 lighthouses, 6 lightships, and 7 offshore lightships which have guided ship captains. Today most of the structures no longer in exist.

Fortunately along the New Jersey coastline, 9 lighthouses remain today: 7 along the Atlantic coast and 2 on the Delaware Bay. These significant historic structures can be visited and several can be climbed. All except one were built in the 19th century.

Each lighthouse in the United States is unique; no two are painted alike although some are similar in design.

The function of a lighthouse is to guide ships into inlets and harbors, and to mark dangers such as rocks and shoals. Few lighthouses remain functional today. Sandy Hook Lighthouse, the oldest lighthouse in the United States, still guides sea captains into New York Harbor. Cape May Lighthouse guards the entrance to Delaware Bay.

ABSECON LIGHTHOUSE
Atlantic City, Atlantic County, NJ

DIRECTIONS: Garden State Parkway to Route 30 (White Horse Pike); drive east into Atlantic City. On Pacific Avenue turn left and follow Vermont or Rhode Island Avenue to the lighthouse.

OPEN: Interior closed to the public.

ABSECON LIGHTHOUSE
Atlantic City, Atlantic County, NJ

Built in 1856, the Absecon Lighthouse, a red banded white spire, was used until 1933. When decommissioned it was replaced by an electric beacon. The keepers house and a United States Life Saving Service Station were destroyed in 1946. In 1946, public outcry fortunately saved the lighthouse.

Absecon Lighthouse, a sister structure to the Barnegat Lighthouse and Cape May Lighthouse, reaches 167 feet above the surf. These lighthouses were designed by Gordon Meade who later gained fame as Union Commander at the Battle of Gettysburg.

As Atlantic City grew, the lighthouse once in a lonely coastal village guiding ships past the dangers of the Absecon and Brigantine shoals, ended up surrounded by neighboring tall buildings.

The Absecon lighthouse was originally built 1300 feet from the waters edge but by 1876 erosion and storms caused the high tide line to be only 75 feet from the lighthouse. At about this time, some jetties 150 feet apart were created in the vicinity of the lighthouse. These were ineffective against winter storms. In 1878, a long jetty was built north of the lighthouse. This provided necessary protection for the light.

In 1893 the colors of the lighthouse were changed to orange and black; since then the lighthouse has been repainted to the original white and red.

In 1932 the light was decommissioned and turned over to the state of New Jersey.

BARNEGAT LIGHTHOUSE
Barnegat Light State Park, Ocean County, NJ

DIRECTIONS: Garden State Parkway to Route 72 East (Exit 63); east on Route 72 to Long Beach Island. Turn left (north) on Long Beach Boulevard and continue to Barnegat Light (9 miles). From Long Beach Boulevard (Central Avenue in Barnegat Light) bear left on Broadway. The entrance to Barnegat Light State Park is on the right at the end of the island.

OPEN: The Lighthouse is open for interior inspection May until September from 10 am until 4:30 pm. Confirm opening times. Call (609) 494-2016. There is no fee for parking. However to tour the lighthouse, the cost is $1.00 per person; children are free.

BARNEGAT LIGHTHOUSE
Barnegat Light State Park, Ocean County, NJ

Barnegat Lighthouse, on the northern tip of Long Beach Island in the fishing village of Barnegat Light, is a magnificent 172 foot red and white spire, known affectionately as 'Old Barney.' Built in 1858 and first lighted on January 1, 1859, 'Old Barney' was not the first lighthouse on this site. Preceded in 1835 by a 40-foot beacon, the lighthouse was claimed by the ocean in 1857.

The present lighthouse, designed by Major George Meade of the Army Corp of Engineers, was completed in 1858 and equipped with a first order Fresnel lens. The last keeper left Barnegat Light in 1926. An automatic light was maintained until 1944. In 1927 the lighthouse function was replaced by the Barnegat Light Ship which has since been decommissioned.

The Barnegat Light Museum, Fifth and Central Avenue, contains the lighthouse lens which was removed in 1927 when the lighthouse was decommissioned. The museum, once the town school, contains other memorabilia of the lighthouse, the fishing industry, and life saving service. Be sure to allow time to visit the Edith Duff Gwinn Gardens which surround the museum.

Barnegat Lighthouse, an imposing structure, has 217 steps to the top of the 170 foot tall tower. The view from the top is worth the long climb. You can even walk out onto the gallery around the lantern. Surrounding the lighthouse is prolific native growth of hollies, bay berries, beach plums, red cedars, sassafras, and beach grass. In the fall, seaside golden rod presents an unforgettable sight. From the park overlooking Barnegat Inlet, one can watch the local fishing fleet leaving and returning to port. Picnic table are available. The lighthouse and grounds are maintained by the State of New Jersey.

CAPE MAY LIGHTHOUSE
Cape May Point, Cape May County, NJ

DIRECTIONS: Garden State Parkway south to the end at Cape May City. Turn onto Lafayette Street and follow Sunset Boulevard. Turn left onto Lighthouse Avenue (Route 629) and follow to the entrance of Cape May Point Sate Park.

OPEN: Admission $3.50 for adults; $1.00 for children. Open during daytime hours from spring through autumn. Restricted winter hours. Call (609) 884-5404 to confirm hours.

CAPE MAY LIGHTHOUSE
Cape May Point, Cape May County, NJ

The Cape May Lighthouse, guarding the entrance to Delaware Bay, is the third lighthouse to be built on the Point. The lighthouse and the town are named after Cornelius Jacobus Mey, an early director of the West India Company.

The first lighthouse was built in 1820, the second in 1847, and the present in 1859. The first two were razed after being threatened and damaged by the sea. The present lighthouse, similar in design to Absecon and Barnegat Lighthouses, is 170 feet tall with a 199 step cast iron spiral staircase, and has walls 8 feet thick at the base.

The lighthouse was electrified in 1933; the lens was removed and placed on display at the Cape May County Historical and Genealogical Museum in Cape May Court House. The lighthouse, still in operation, is now equipped with a 36 inch hyper-radial lens.

The Mid-Atlantic Center for the Arts received a license for this historic Cape May Lighthouse from the State of New Jersey. In 1988 the lighthouse was opened for tours. Plans are to install an interpretative center and acquire artifacts. In 1990 the 1893 oil storage house exterior was restored to its original appearance. The interior was converted to a gift shop and visitors center.

Visitors can climb the lighthouses' 199 spiral steps for a spectacular view of the Atlantic coast.

Contributions for restoration and acquisition of artifacts may be made to the Mid-Atlantic Center for the Arts, PO Box 340, Cape May, NJ 08204.

EAST POINT LIGHTHOUSE
East Point, Cumberland County, NJ
(or MAURICE RIVER LIGHTHOUSE)

DIRECTIONS: Garden State Parkway to Exit 4. Turn off the Parkway onto Route 47 West. Follow Route 47 to Dennisville. After Dennisville Route 47 becomes Delsea Drive. Follow this to Delmont. After Delmont turn left toward Heislerville. Turn left onto East Point Road. Follow it to the Bay. East Point Lighthouse is on the right side of the beach.

OPEN: No regular hours. Group tours may be arranged. Free. Phone (609) 825-3386 for information.

EAST POINT LIGHTHOUSE
(or MAURICE RIVER LIGHTHOUSE)
East Point, Cumberland County, NJ

The East Point Lighthouse or Maurice River Lighthouse, as it is frequently called, was build in 1849 on the point of land that juts into the Delaware Bay between Thompson's Beach and the mouth of the Maurice River to guide mariners away from Dead Mans Shoal and into the entrance channel of the Maurice River.

This picturesque brick structure is a two and one-half story house with a cupola dominating the marsh grasses southeast of the village of Heislerville. Operated until 1941 when the Coast Guard abandoned it, in 1956 it was licensed to the state and in 1971 was acquired by the Maurice River Historical Society as a site for a museum. Since then it has been the subject of much vandalism.

Presently the East Point Lighthouse is being restored by the Maurice River Historical Society.

FORT MOTT LIGHTHOUSE
(or FINNS POINT REAR RANGE LIGHT)
Pennsville, Salem County, NJ

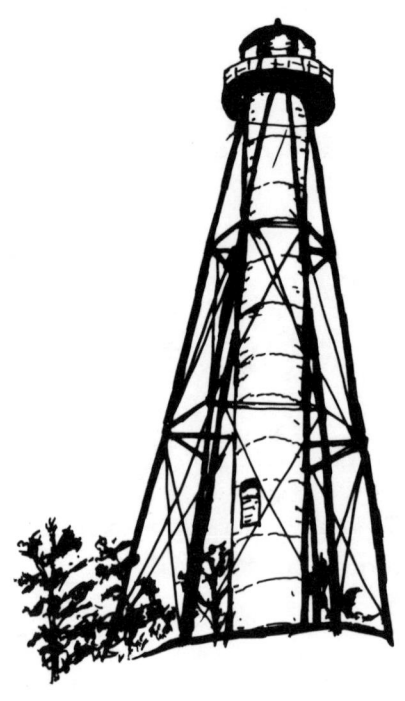

DIRECTIONS: Garden State Parkway to Exit 4. Turn off the Parkway onto Route 47 W. Take Route 47 to Millville where it becomes Port Elizabeth Road. In Millville take the Bridgeton-Millville Road which becomes Route 49 West. Follow Route 49 to Pennsville. Turn left on either Lighthouse Road or follow signs to Fort Mott State Park. The Fort Mott Lighthouse is a short distance before the Fort at the "Y" in the road.

OPEN: Open 12 noon to 4 pm on the 3rd Sunday of every month except in winter. Free.

FORT MOTT LIGHTHOUSE
(or FINNS POINT REAR RANGE LIGHT)
Pennsville, Salem County, NJ

Located in the Supawna Meadows in the Tinicum National Environmental Center Refuge, the Fort Mott Lighthouse overlooks the Delaware Bay south of Pennsville and west of Salem. Built in 1876, this lighthouse is a 105-foot tower with 127 steps, featuring rare wrought-iron work and a Greek Revival doorway. The keeper lived in a house beside the light. This site for a lighthouse was chosen to mark the river channel from Bombay Hook to Reedy Point.

In 1939 the Fort Mott lighthouse was automated and continued operation until March 22, 1950. The US Coast Guard declared it excess property in 1951 because of changes in the river channel. In the 1950's it became part of the National Wildlife Refuge. During the following years, it was subject to much vandalism including burning of the keepers house in 1978. Today only a part of the shed remains of the original buildings. In 1978 the lighthouse was added to the National Register of Historic places.

In 1981 a "Save the Lighthouse Committee" was formed and through diligent work was able to secure funds for restoring the lighthouse. In 1983 restoration was completed. The fate of the lighthouse as well as its availability to the public is undecided. There is a fascinating fort nearby plus picnic facilities.

HEREFORD INLET LIGHTHOUSE
North Wildwood, Cape May County, NJ

DIRECTIONS: Garden State Parkway to Exit 8, Route 147. Follow Route 147 into North Wildwood. The Hereford Inlet Lighthouse is next to the Coast Guard Station at the south side of Hereford Inlet at First Street and Central Avenue.

OPEN: June 12 to Sept 18; hours 9 am to 5 pm, Monday-Thursday and Saturday; 9 am to 8 pm on Friday and 12 noon to 4 pm on Sunday. Free. Confirm hours (609) 522-4520.

HEREFORD INLET LIGHTHOUSE
North Wildwood, Cape May County, NJ

The Hereford Inlet Lighthouse was authorized by Congress in 1872. This quaint Victorian structure, lighted in 1874, is one of the most unusual and attractive of New Jersey's lighthouses. Its two stories are topped by a light tower for a total of 46 feet.

The structure is a sister to four others constructed in California of which two remain (East Brother Island and Point Fermin) and one in Oregon, long removed.

In 1913 a severe storm washed out much of the beach undermining the foundation of the Hereford Light. The building was then physically moved west about 150 feet.

Decommissioned in 1963, the Coast Guard transferred the property to the New Jersey Marine Police, removed the optic, and abandoned the structure. In 1977 the lighthouse was registered in the State and National Registers of Historic Places. In 1982 the City of North Wildwood took over the Hereford Lighthouse for use as an information center and maritime museum. Hard working loyal citizens are restoring the lighthouse to its original splendor.

In 1984 the lighthouse was open to visitors, and in 1986 the Coast Guard relocated the Hereford Inlet optic back into the lantern room where it flashes today as an aid to navigation. One of the old fourth Order Fresnel lenses is on display on the first floor.

The Hereford Inlet Lighthouse Commission continues to improve the light and grounds. Those wishing to aid this project may send their contributions to the Hereford Lighthouse Restoration, PO Box 499, North Wildwood, NJ 08260.

SANDY HOOK LIGHTHOUSE
Gateway National Recreation Area,
Monmouth County, NJ

DIRECTIONS: Garden State Parkway to Exit 117. Follow Route 36 over the Highlands Bridge and follow signs to the Gateway National Recreation Area, Sandy Hook. Follow signs in the park to the lighthouse. Be sure to stop at the Spermaceti Cove Visitors Center to see the exhibits and pick up tour information. Visit Historic Fort Hancock and the museum in the post jail.

OPEN: Grounds open daily from 9 am to 4 pm. Call (201) 872-0115 to confirm or write to Sandy Hook Unit, Gateway NRA, PO box 530, Fort Hancock, NJ 07732.

SANDY HOOK LIGHTHOUSE
Gateway National Recreation Area,
Monmouth County, NJ

Sandy Hook Lighthouse, the fifth light tower build in colonial America, is the oldest operating lighthouse in the nation. Although the interior is closed to the public, one can tour the grounds and admire the architecture. In operation since June 11, 1764, the Sandy Hook Light, originally called the New York Lighthouse, was built by a group of New York merchants to avert shipping disasters. It was one of the 12 lighthouses built by the colonies which were later ceded to the United States.

The Sandy Hook Light, overlooking New York Bay, is white with eight equal sides; the diameter of the base is 29 feet and at the top of the wall, 15 feet. The circumference is 33 feet. The lighthouse is nine stories, that is, 103 feet from bottom to top. Now a National Historic Landmark, it was automated in the early 1960's.

The light is a 60,000 candlepower, third-order Fresnel lens installed in 1856 and is still in use today. The light is a fixed (nonblinking) white, 85 feet above ground and 88 feet above water, visible for 19 miles on a clear night.

During the American Revolution, the lighthouse was strategic. British loyalists fortified the structure and used it as a base for raids on local farms and towns. American forces were unsuccessful in attempting to destroy it. Although revolutionary battles raged around it, the masonry tower survives to this day.

During World War II, the Sandy Hook Light was extinguished to protect New York Harbor. The light, automated in 1962, today continues to guide mariners into New York Harbor. The lighthouse, located on National Park Service property, is within the confines of Fort Hancock and is owned and maintained by the US Coast Guard.

A group has been formed to preserve the lighthouse and related artifacts. Contributions may be made to the Sandy Hook Chapter of the USLAS, c/o Coast Guard, Sandy Hook, NJ 07732.

SEA GIRT LIGHTHOUSE
Sea Girt, Monmouth County, NJ

DIRECTIONS: Garden State Parkway to Exit 98 (Route 36 East). Continue on Route 138 to Route 71 into Sea Girt. The lighthouse is on Beacon Boulevard and First Street.

OPEN: Open periodically. Free. For information call (908) 449-5056.

SEA GIRT LIGHTHOUSE
Sea Girt, Monmouth County, NJ

Built in 1896, the Victorian Sea Girt Lighthouse is unusual. Its square turret rises from a compact, two story, L-shaped brick house that faces Beacon Boulevard. The turret is 60 feet above the high water mark. Sea Girt was chosen as a site for a lighthouse because it is midway between Sandy Hook and Barnegat Lighthouses, a distance of some 38 miles.

During World War II, the Sea Girt Light was occupied by the Coast Guard, serving as an observation post to guard against Nazi agents who might come by submarine.

In 1921 it became the first lighthouse to be equipped with a radio fog signal. The Sea Girt Light was equipped with a fourth order Fresnel lens showing a flashing red light every 6 seconds.

Sea Girt Lighthouse was decommissioned in 1945 and bought by the Borough of Sea Girt in 1956. The lighthouse was used for a time as a recreation center and in 1981 came under the care of the Sea Girt Lighthouse Commission. Since 1981 the lighthouse has been refurbished and maintained by the this group.

TWIN LIGHTS OF THE NAVESINK
Highlands, Monmouth County, NJ

DIRECTIONS: Garden State Parkway to Exit 117. Follow Route 36 toward the bridge but turn right before the bridge on Portland Road and take an immediate right on Lighthouse Drive. Proceed to the site entrance on the left. Beware! This is a narrow curved road that is best suited for mountain goats! The sight is worth the treacherous drive.

OPEN: Daily 9 am to 5 pm. Free. (908) 872-1814

TWIN LIGHTS OF THE NAVESINK
Highlands, Monmouth County, NJ

The Twin Lights of the Navesink, a fortress-like structure, consists of two brownstone towers connected by a 228 foot dwelling. The towers, 256 feet above sea level, situated in the Highlands of the Navesink, mark the westerly side of the entrance to New York Harbor. Not really twins, the south tower is square with 65 steps, while the north one is octagonal with 64 steps. The north tower was officially named Navesink Light. Why the two towers differ is a mystery. The south tower contained the first Fourth order Fresnel lens in the United States. The north tower was lit by a lens of the Second order, indicating to ships they were coming up on a headland along the seacoast and the approach to a bay.

The present lights were built on the Highlands in 1862. These lights replaced an earlier unconnected pair of towers that had stood since 1828. The present lights were the first in the United States to be equipped with a 7-foot Fresnel lens and the first to be electrically powered. They were the most powerful in the county; the lights themselves were visible 22 miles out to sea, while their glow ranged outward 70 miles. According to some authorities, it was not the torch of Lady Liberty that our forebears first saw, but the blaze of these majestic lights.

The light station was decommissioned in 1949 by the United States Coast Guard. The lights were last lit in 1952. In 1960 the station was added to the list of New Jersey Sate Historic Sites. At present the facility houses a fine collection of US Life Saving Service memorabilia and boats of the New Jersey shore such as the Barnegat Sneak Box, the Sea Bright Beach Skiff, and the Shrewsbury Crab Skiff. A replica of the original wireless telegraph equipment used by Marconi in 1899 is on display.

On a clear day, the view from the grounds is one of the most spectacular along the East coast. One sees a sweeping vista of Sandy Hook, the bay, the ocean, and the New York skyline. One can also see Sandy Hook Lighthouse, Ambrose Light Tower, as well as the Romer Shoal and West Bank Lighthouses in New York waters.

For those interested in additional information about lighthouses, the author suggests you contact the following organizations:

The United States Lighthouse Society
244 Kearny St, 5th Floor
San Francisco, Ca 94108

Lighthouse Preservation Society
Box 736
Rockport, MA 01966

Office of New Jersey Heritage
State Parks Service
Trenton, NJ 08625

New Jersey Division of Travel & Tourism
CN 826
Trenton, NJ 08625

Lighthouse Digest
PO Box 1690
Wells, ME 04090

* Remember,
August is NATIONAL LIGHTHOUSE month.
* *

Other books by the author include
- A Guide to New Jersey's Lighthouses $4.95
- Gardening on the Eastern Seashore $12.95
- Seashore Plants by Mail $5.95
- Cranberry Cookery $7.95
- Flavored Vinegars: Herb and Fruit $6.95
- Herb Sauces, Salsas, and Such $6.95
- SIMPLY SHRIMP! $8.95
- Seafood Smoking $5.95
- Bargain Seafoods: Cooking the Underutilized Species A$7.95
- Seafood Secrets: A Nutritional Guide to Seafood $9.95
- The SIMPLY SEAFOOD COOKBOOK...of East Coast Shellfish $8.95
- Mustard Magic! $6.95
- The Best of Blueberries $7.95

To order by mail, please include $2.00 for postage and handling. NJ residents, please add 6% for sales tax.

SEND TO
BARNEGAT LIGHT PRESS
PO Box 305, 26 West Third Street
Barnegat Light, NJ 08006